The Magnificent Seven Do Cayucos

AMY LYKOSH

MAKARIOS
PRESS

MAKARIOS PRESS

O

Contents

Friday, April 4, 2025

Wednesday, April 2, 2025

Early Alarm

I had set my alarm for 2:30am,
    But when Phil's alarm went off at 2:10,
    I thought about all the things I had remembered
    I yet needed to do when I was falling asleep,
    And decided to get up.

    It was a prudent decision.
    I worked all the minutes
    Until our on-time departure at 2:45am.

Do You Have Anything That Might Be a Problem?

Phil asked Isaiah, and asked him again:

"Do you have anything in your bag that might be a problem?"

"I don't think so," Isaiah answered
Unconvincingly.

"Look again."

"Oh! Here's another lighter I forgot."

Almost the Wrong House

When we drove up to Jadon's house
    Shortly before 3:30am,
    His light was on.

Joe jumped out to let him know we'd arrived.

"No!" yelled Phil, very loudly.

Joe was about to rap on the door of the wrong house.

No matter.
Jadon came out.

A Second Double-Check

"Caleb, do you have your pocket knife still?"

"Oh ... yes."

"Leave it in the car."

No Need to Arrive Early

As I suspected might be the case,
　　The airport security was still shut down at 3:50am.
　　After a brief wait, the mass of twelve people
　　Surged toward security.

We Were Right to Be Unconvinced

Turns out that a straight-edge razor
   Is considered hazardous.

   Phil's conscience was clear.
   He had mentioned this before.

   Isaiah was escorted out the exit,
   Handed back his blade to dispose of elsewhere.

   He circled back through security,
   Then caught up with us.

Status

Because Phil and Joe needed another flight back,
    I couldn't exercise my Priority Status
    For them, too.

    They boarded in Group 7
    (Or something even worse),
    Heading to the back of the plane.

First Time All on the Same Plane in ... a While

I was trying to remember when we all flew together.

Maybe on the way back from Family Fun Week 2020,

When we all returned from Colorado.

But the last time we flew out on a trip together:

I think maybe Belize 2017.

What the Pilot Sees

As we prepared to take off,
   I could look out the window briefly
   To see the runway lights illumine the darkness.

Concourse E

When we landed in Charlotte,
    Bob wasn't quite ready to pray
    (I had said: 6:45, unless we land early …
    And we landed early).

    I threw Abraham off by heading the wrong direction—
    Eager to see what construction progress,
    What prayer space I normally inhabit—
    But all was mostly well.

Concourse D

I have rarely gone to Concourse D.
   It's stubby and uninteresting.

   A girl in a hoodie, yoga pants, and stiletto heels ...
   At 6:30am.

   Another hefty, plain girl, clingy to her man,
   Wearing a bare midrift shirt and mermaid jeans.

   Jesus knows the stories of all of these unusual ones,
   And loves each one.

Person Shuffle

When I chose seats for the long flight,
  Charlotte to Phoenix,
  I wasn't sure if Phil would pay extra for his seats,
  So I chose an aisle for Phil,
  A middle for me,
  A window for Caleb,
  Plus a window in front
  And a window behind.

But Phil bought his own seats.

Caleb, pleased, said, "I have two windows!"
Abraham protested, "I have only part of one window!"

So I swapped.

Three boys in front of me,
And one more in front of them.

A happy place.

After Three and a Half Hours of Sleep

I vaguely remember takeoff,
  And then, blissful, sleep.
  I think I finally woke up, to be up, at 9:15am.

Productive

I had my last spurt of productivity for days
    As I was flying to Phoenix.
    I had the idea for a creative series for a month:
    How to Pray for Business the Workplace Prayer Way.

    A few hours of independent work time
    Allowed me time to pull together the disparate bits
    From here and there.

Phoenix

I think our family drove through in 2017
　　On our way to Ken's funeral.

　　I have a vague memory of
　　Stopping for gas at a seedy station.

　　We were surprised by a mountain of dirt
　　In the middle of four skyscrapers,

　　And the river of water that seemed to
　　Start and stop on a whim.

Needed Relief on a Short Layover

Although our flight seemed to leave on time,
  Somehow we landed, I think, a bit late ...
  Only fifteen minutes until boarding.
  (Bob said later: massive storms throughout
  Tornado Alley.)

  We speed-walked through the airport,
  Bladders in pain,
  Reached our gate with four minutes until boarding.
  Just enough time to go.

Miscalculation

In retrospect, this was too much in too little a time.
   I decided to send Bob the file,
   So excited, and uncertain how soon we would
   Have internet again.

   After the minute or two, I looked up to board ...
   To find no sons around me.

   Still in the bathroom? Already boarded?

   By the time enough of us assembled,
   The boarding window for Group 4 had closed.

   All remaining bags: gate-checked.
   Three of the four.

   Heartsick.

Next Time I'll Know Better

I left my rollerboard on the bridgeway.
   I shouldn't have.
   The overhead bins were empty.

   But someone was sitting in my seat,
   And by the time I got back to the front,
   My bag was gone.

   And if one bag is gone,
   All three might as well be.
   No one died, but it was a moment of chaos.

Flight Attendant Game of Tag

The flight attendant at the front of the plane said,
    "Oh! You're our Priority passenger."
    Indeed.

    He sent me to the back to the back of the plane.
    That flight attendant had no idea what to do.
    He muddled through, though.

Precious Compensation

I eventually ended up
   Not with a window seat,

   But next to Caleb,
   Who periodically would give me

   A little love pat.

Two Books on Finances

I finished Luther Blackwell's book
   Power to Get Wealth, and
   Mitzi Purdue's
   How to Make Your Family Business Last.

I only brought finance books,
But how satisfying.
This is a game I can start to play.

Distress

Caleb started to feel queasy as we came in for a landing.
    The approach, over the hills of California, was bouncy.

    Isaiah got sudden shooting pain in his eye,
    Perhaps sinus pressure from the head cold that struck him.

    But we arrived with neither vomiting,
    So I'll count that as a win.

Rental Cars

Phil went to Avis for his car.
   I went to Enterprise for my car.

   I would return my car to the same location,
   While Phil was returning his elsewhere.

   Not all rental car agencies are set up to do that.

   I would have tried to figure out how to
   Fit everyone in one car.

   Phil's idea was much better.

We Waited and Waited

Our luggage, taken from us,
   Seemed to be returned
   Only against the will of the airport.

   Phil and the boys talked about
   Their favorite character in *Dune*.
   I read a book and pretended
   This delay wasn't happening.

   I will attempt to never surrender my luggage again,
   Unless a flight attendant forces me.

Going to Whole Foods

After our bags arrived,
    I was ready to go to Whole Foods.
    We would get food for lunch
    And pick up our order.

    I thought Phil was going for coffee,
    And laughed when I saw the Starbucks
    Across the parking lot.

    But he surprised me in the prepared food section
    Only a minute or two after we arrived.

The Pastry Counter

"Are you eyeing the cheesecake?
   Yeah, me, too," Phil said to a son,
   Then walked away.

   It was a beauty.

Cake Numbers

As the pastry clerk handed over a large box,
   I asked for a flourless chocolate cake as well.

Caleb said, "Mom, that's so odd: 1, 1, 1, 2, 3 ...
What are those numbers?"

"Those are birthday candles to celebrate
A specific birthday, like 5, 0 for 50."

"Can we do that, too?"

Ah. Yes. Good thinking.

Finally

By the time all six selected food and drinks,
    I am pretty sure we could have
    Waited in line, ordered, and eaten at Chipotle.

    The tyranny of too many choices.

Second Checkout

While the boys ate,
   I bought
   A bag of oranges,
   Two apples,
   Fifty-six paper plates,
   A few paper cups,
   Six boxes LaCroix sparkling water,
   One pack bottled water,
   Two packs plastic forks.

I could tell that my brain was tired,
As I felt like I was processing slowly.

And I didn't want to buy more food
Until we determined how much
Catering was coming.

Catering Pickup

I went to announce my arrival.

"Be prepared for six or seven carts."

Oh, goodness.

Space Management

Phil had already been planning:

If we shift all luggage to one car,
Five can ride,

While we put the seats down for food,
With two people, in the other car.

This genius plan proved successful.

A Mountain of Food

I had tried to buy, as led by the Spirit.
    When I told Phil it was $1600, he first said:
    "That's not bad" ...
    Then revised:
    "But a bit much for lunch."

    I had thought:
    Pinwheel sandwiches for sixteen, times three ...
    But that's not a meal.

And it's not.

But the food kept coming and coming.

And it all needed to be refrigerated.

This Was a Great Kindness

Phil said nothing,
   As tray after tray
   Loaded into the car.

Sympathy

I remember counting off the items,
    Ensuring we weren't forgetting any tray.

    "I hope this is for a happy occasion?"
    The head of catering trailed off uncertainly.

    "Well ... it's a celebration of life,
    Which is happy in its own way," I replied.

    She winced.
    "I thought that might be the case. I'm so sorry."

Uncertainty

We would drive to Cayucos,

    To sort through this unbelievable quantity of food.

    I prayed aloud for wisdom.

    As we drove I thought:

    "We can separate out what seems like a reasonable amount,

    And try to store it in the church refrigerator.

    What's left, we can take back to the house.

    I can put some in bags to store in the fridge."

Specific Instructions for Me

Though I normally avoid American wheat products,

    I felt a specific, unexpected invitation:

    Almost everything has wheat.

    Eat what you will as you are away.

A Few Memories

Jadon happily admitted to always being willing
   To eat the last cookie or piece of cake.

   I shared about the one time I ate the last shrimp,
   Only to hear, a few minutes later, the host,
   Furious, wondering where the last shrimp had gone.
   (The only time in almost 50 years
   This strategy had failed me.)

   A few stories to tell as we drove the green rolling hills
   Of the central California coast.

   Jadon remembered getting carsick
   As we drove to Cayucos.
   (When would this have been? Ken's funeral?)

   And then ... the ocean!

Unbelievable Kindness

We unloaded the car into the kitchen.

The top of the island shifted,
But Joe managed to catch two trays
So they didn't end up on the floor.

Phil and the organizer Lisa stepped out,
To let me rearrange.

What would be good for Friday?
What was excessive and could go?

We were trying to plan for about 40.
If my family of seven ate six meals,
How much food would that be?

Once we had a good general sense,
Phil and Lisa gave some additional feedback.

And the church refrigerator was industrial size!

Unlike the home-size in our current church,
Or the no-refrigerator-because-we-meet-in-a-school
Of the two churches before that.

I actually have no idea what we would have done
If we had received all this food in a normal-sized fridge.

I could do nothing but offer grateful thanks to God.

Adulting

The beach felt like dirty sand.

    I was cold.

    The wind blew hard.

    Would I be warmer at all before I returned to Virginia?

    Phil was pleased to be back.

    I saw little of beauty,

    But tried to keep the grumpiness in check.

Hooray for Tourists

The giant-sized turquoise
  Adirondack chair near the boardwalk—
  A typical photo op.

  Which we definitely took advantage of.

No Entry Before Four

I had asked for clemency with the hosts,
    But their cleaning crew wasn't done at 3pm.
    Phil drove us to the beach.
    Caleb, still queasy, dozed in the car.
    Phil went into a candy store to get a coffee,
    While we admired the candy of my youth:
    Laffy Taffy, Lemonheads, Smarties, candy necklaces.

    Then we walked out on the pier, as far as allowed—
    The end blocked off, in need of maintenance, unsafe.

    We were just biding time.
    Until, at last, it was time!

Pay Attention to the Double Takes

As we drove, we passed
   A bush with purple rockets,
   Backlit and stunning.

Paradise Awaits Through These Double Doors

The outer door to an enclosed breezeway.
    A lockbox with two keys.

    Open the first door
    To a glorious patch of green grass,
    Flowers, sunken patio,

    Only dimly noticed.

The Redwoods and Glass House

Iconic house, designed by local architect George Nagano,
    Cantilevered over a crumbling rock,
    The 270-degree view of the ocean surprised and delighted us
    Every time we caught a glimpse.

    I took a glance,
    Then turned my attention to dealing with the food.

Ziploc Blessing

I don't remember ever being in a rental house
    With gallon-sized Ziplocs.

Sometimes sandwich bags ... maybe.

I almost cried when, on edge and exhausted,
I opened a drawer to find some gallon-sized Ziplocs.

For almost two hours, I worked in the kitchen:
Putting shrimp in bags,
Offering sushi to boys,
Combining sauces in tubs,
Putting olives here and there,
Combining pinwheels for better storage.

Jennifer stopped by.
I greeted her, fed a nephew a sushi or two,
Kept working.

Chantilly Cake

I had ordered a cake to serve 20,
   Full of berries and whipped cream,
   With, apparently, a light almond flavor.

   We took one for us.

   I had only a few tiny tastes,
   But we ate the first half in ecstatic
   Thanksgiving.

On My Way Upstairs

I was arrested by the vertical window at the staircase landing:

    Perfectly situated to look down the beach to Morro Rock.

    This sort of unexpected perfection

    Didn't happen by accident—

    A blessing of creativity and wisdom by the architect and builder.

So Thankful I Don't Own This House

As beautiful and unique as this house is,
    The vague smell of mildew reminded me:
    How intense it is to maintain anything.

    The window on the stairwell to the south: fine.
    The windows on the stairwell to the north: not fine.

    Not only were they streaky, but the amount of air
    Blowing in through the edge
    Was enough to almost toss my hair.

    A gift to stay for a few days,
    Then turn back to the owner.

When It Was Almost Six

I walked around the house.
  It was nice.

  I went to my bedroom.
  It had a skylight above the headboard.

  I think I was asleep by 6:30pm.

  I heard reports later that
  Phil had watched the sunset,
  The boys had watched a movie.

  But I knew nothing of that.
  This mama was tired.

Thursday, April 3, 2025

That 4am Wakeup Call

I had plugged my phone in across the room.
   The first time I started awake,
   It was around midnight.
   I had already been asleep almost a full night.

   I fell asleep again,
   And was incredibly disoriented
   When I woke at 4am.

   I didn't want to walk in the pitch darkness,
   In the howling wind ...

   But the Lord reminded me
   Of the garage.

   So I spent a groggy hour in prayer,
   Then another half hour.

   Afterward I think I greeted Caleb and Phil,
   Ate some shrimp,

Then went back to bed.

Was it 11:15am when I awoke?

In Virginia, yes, it was!

Sleeping Arrangements

Jadon slept on the couch in an sitting room.
    He could have pulled out the hide-a-bed, but didn't.

Next Joe took a room with a queen bed.

Isaiah took a room with a single,
But a large desk.
He was the only one of us to spend much time in his room,
So the room fit.

Finally, Caleb on the top bunk,
Abraham on the queen bed below.

Now that Jadon moved out, only four boys in one room ...
But when they get a chance, they happily spread out.

The Limits of Cell Phone Cameras

I woke to find the shutters in my room open,
    The ocean visible from where I lay in bed.
    Astonishing.

    To take a photo of this wonder:
    Impossible.
    Too strong a contrast between the dark and the light.

Saturated Seaweed

Caleb and I headed down to the beach.
  He found a long, gourd-like seaweed.
  When he stepped on it, it squirted.

  So he stepped on it again and again,
  Until he had emptied it.

Let's Go for a Walk!

Phil made a mention that,
   While I was sleeping,
   He and Caleb had walked
   "Not quite to the pier, but close."

"Come on, boys! Let's walk!"

Caleb was, perhaps, fatigued,
And Abraham said, "My shins are cold."
They turned back.

But Joe and I went out for a walk
In the sun, wind, and surf.

We reached the pier.

Retaining Walls

On our walk north,

    We noticed the wide range of retaining walls,

    Keeping the ocean-front homes

    From collapsing into the sea.

    Each house had its own, unique method.

    Sometimes I walk neighborhoods,

    Admiring gardens or architecture.

    This was the first time I admired

Retaining walls.

Pier Closed for Maintenance

How handy that we walked the pier when we arrived ...

    This day it was closed for maintenance ...

    Though not a worker was in sight.

The Return Walk

The sun and the angle obscured the houses,
    But we admired the view ...
    Sort of.

    We compared footprints in the sand.
    Surely somewhere an FBI database
    Holds a record of the bottoms of shoes.

    I wondered at one point about seaglass,
    And wondered if I'd found a piece.
    (It might have been a translucent rock.)

    But we chatted and chuckled
    As we walked along the pebbles and firm sand
    Of the beach my husband loves.

The Other Half of Chantilly

I left Phil talking on the phone.
    I had cut six more large pieces of cake,
    Leaving a bit on the end,
    To perhaps eat when I returned.

    But when it was all gone …
    No harm, no foul.

The few tastes were sufficient.

Will the Food Hold?

I noticed the browning of the avocado in sushi.
   I felt the slight sogginess of the pinwheels and cheese blocks ...
   Condensation on platters was one thing I could not control.

(*Lord, protect the food.*)

The Koi Puzzle

I brought one Liberty Puzzle
   I had never done,
   Two brilliant orange koi
   Swimming in a blue-green background,
   Far too much for me to tackle on my own.
   But with the family, I had hope.

Always Limited Time

I wrastled the family together,
 Uncomfortably forcing all to participate
 In a conversation about
 Giving, investing, family bank.

 It started out a bit rough,
 Heading down a side path or two,
 But in the end, we talked for a while,
 And talked again,
 Discussing the challenges of giving.

 Phil took a bathroom break, and
 We almost scattered,
 But I called us together again,
 To talk briefly about investing,

Until we were well and truly done.

I celebrated my unmutedness.

Happiest Observation

At one point,
    Commiserating about our shared antipathy
    For things much of the world finds delightful
    (Was the topic this time Abraham Lincoln?),
    Isaiah said happily,
    "I love our family."

Caleb, Recovering

Caleb lay under a blanket on the stairs
   During our full conversation.
   He wasn't just being a pill.
   His stomach was still unsettled.

   I volunteered to stay with him in the afternoon.

Cobble Street Cousins

Caleb and I read an early reader,

    In which three cousins form a cookie company

    And make some new friends with their early customers.

Answering All the Wishes I Can

Caleb noticed a frosted rice crispy treat,
    Covered in natural colored sprinkles.
    It was sugar on sugar,
    But promised to be delicious.

    He didn't ask for it,
    But I bought it.

    I shared it: two-thirds for him,
    One-third for the rest of us.

    When I took my bite,
    My eyes went wide:
    This was about the sweetest thing
    I've ever put in my mouth. Wow!

    But when Phil declined his,
    I happily claimed the last piece.

At the Church

Phil directed the boys as they
    Set up tables,
    Arranged chairs,
    Set out the tablecloths,
    Rearranged chairs,

    Preparing the space
    To hold space.

Elephant Seals

The family stopped off at home
    With an invitation:

    "Want to see elephant seals?
    Abraham's staying home."

    I had seen elephant seals before,
    Like giant, smelly slugs.

    I gratefully stayed in with Abraham,
    Though Caleb headed out.

The Cayucos Memory Tour

Phil took the boys to see
 The house Uncle Mark built,
 Where his family stayed on Thanksgiving,
 The children in sleeping bags on the floor.

During the Elephant Seal Excursion

I kept thinking: I should do something productive.
　　But louder than that urge:
　　Finish the puzzle.

　　So I did.

　　Beautiful shades of grey-green,
　　Almost luminescent.

Visitors One, Two, Three

A seagull landed on the deck railing
  And stood, head cocked, head raised,
  Complaining and calling.

  Abraham took a picture.
  He texted the family:
  "You may have seen elephant seals,
  But Mom and I saw some wildlife, too."

  A minute later, a second seagull landed,
  And they stood, heads cocked, heads raised,
  Complaining and calling.

  Abraham took a picture.
  "Oh no, they're amassing an army!"

  A minute later, a third seagull landed,
  And they stood, heads cocked, heads raised,
  Complaining and calling.

Abraham took a picture.

"They're talking! Does anyone know seagullese?!"

Jadon sent back a meme with a colony of seagulls
And the words: "Mine! Mine! Mine! Mine!"

"Perfect! Not the most reassuring though...."

A Full Fridge of Prepared Food

With all catered food,
    The most I had to do in the kitchen
    All day was open a bag or cut a slice and
    Eat.

    I'm not sure I would describe it as restful—
    But it sure is different!

Thinking About Sudden Wealth

With Phil's mom's passing, he came into an inheritance.

Not enough to stop working,

But the largest single gift we have ever received.

He has, thus far, done nothing with it.

In *The Sudden Wealth Solution*,

The author discusses inheritance and other sudden payouts.

He recommends we think about our financial goals—

A task I had never once considered.

But this seemed like a good assignment,

So in the quiet house, I thought of mine.

Amy's Goals for Wealth

• Always practice hearing the voice of God

  • Enough financial independence that I can live my days as I do now: adding to my body of work, enjoying learning

  • Occasional vacations to places I want to go: Mackinac Island, the iconic house in Cayucos, Amsterdam, etc.

  • Inheritance to the children (or, as Phil would say: the grandchildren)

  • Ability to not be a burden to the children—money for care for both of us, should this matter

  • Only investing in companies that keep our consciences clear

  • Generosity

  • Some form of world change with our finances—that would be so cool!

  • Life-building partnerships, instead of life-sucking partnerships

A Question

"Do we need ice cream?"
    And a photo of a freezer of Haagen Dazs.

Ah, Isaiah, this is a good question.
Clearly, our freezer has none.

And while "need" might be a bit of a stretch,
Given how much food our refrigerator has,

What is the point of a vacation
If we can't enjoy some fun flavors.

Yes. We need ice cream.
Vanilla, strawberry, raspberry sorbet, mint chip, dulce de leche.

Starting the Puzzle a Second Time

I broke the finished puzzle into bits,
    Then, as we talked together, I started it again.
    I didn't get very far.

The Last Game for One of the Players

I could hear Caleb's frustration,
    And after he lost again,
    I sent him to bed.

    It was only 6:45pm,
    But he was up hours earlier than his brothers,
    And who knows how late he had gone to bed?

    Tonight: back to sleep at a normal (Virginia) time.

High(er) Tide

I tried to walk the beach,
    But the tide was in,
    Making most of the beach impassable.

    After a few minutes, I headed back.
    I could enjoy the view and the light
    From the comfort of indoors.

Sunset

Though Caleb was asleep,
  The rest of us gathered at 7:15pm
  To watch the sunset over the water.

  A low-lying cloud, far out over the water,
  Obscured the actual sun sinking into the sea,
  But it was orange and beautiful,

  A pause for a few minutes to
  Simply observe the daily occurrence.

  And then I was ready for bed.

After I Went to Bed

I had made it until almost 7:45pm,
    But the night was yet young for the boys.
    Ice cream, games ... lots of things!

Friday, April 4, 2025

Another Early Morning Rising Time

Multiple times through the night,
    I drifted in and out of sleep, thinking about a college.

    I awoke around 4am, with a cutting sore throat.
    Good thing I travel with homeopathy.

    I woke early enough to work by computer light
    In the bathroom, thinking about possible courses.

    I washed my hair by the finicky shower flow,
    Taming the wild mane of travel and beach.

    By the time prayer time began,
    I was in the garage and ready to go.

The Turning Point

Caleb, Phil, and I set out to walk to the pier.
   Phil mentioned that he had talked to a man
   Who was looking for seaglass.

   Caleb had found three pieces the day before.
   This was Phil's birthday—maybe we could find some.

   Almost immediately,
   Phil and Caleb started finding pieces.
   So did I.

   Caleb found
   Blue and green and yellow-green, clear and brown.

   My collection was not as colorful,
   Only clear and green and brown,
   But a few larger pieces, too.

   More than fifty bits for me by the end of the walk,
   And more again for Caleb,

Like little jewels or Easter eggs,
Scattered for me on the beach on Phil's birthday.

The wind had died down, and the beach was beautiful.
I turned from dislike to appreciation.

Take What You Want—It Won't Be There Later

"Every tide there are new deposits.
   The beach is covered with the stuff."

   A friendly man walking by
   Commented on the unanticipated abundance.

Five Minutes Out

I looked ahead at the pier.
"I think we're five minutes out."

Phil checked his phone.
"Google Maps says 11 minutes out."

Caleb started timing us.
We were 12 minutes, 12 seconds out.

The Coffee Shop

We stopped by a coffee shop.
    It was Phil's birthday, after all.
    What would he like?

    Hot chocolate for Caleb.
    Vanilla latte for Phil.
    Chai steamer for me.

Getting Bearings

"Was this the old arcade?"
  Phil asked the barista, a long-time local.
  She wasn't sure.
  But she knew of Mr. Kniffen,
  The middle school teacher,
  Though she didn't think she ever had him.

Everyone knows Mr. Kniffen.

As we walked further down the block,
Sipping drinks,
Phil was pretty sure he found the old arcade,
Now Hidden Kitchen,
Specializing in sweet and savory blue corn waffles.

An Annual Event?

Phil said, "I could see coming here every year,
 In April, when the hills are still green."
 "But what would you *do*?"
 "I don't know—I just like the view."

 After discovering the replenishing treasure of seaglass,
 I could imagine (sort of)
 Returning, year after year,
 For a week of reading and puzzles,
 Slow walks and chai tea.

From the AirBnb Description

Cayucos by-the-Sea is located on
    California's scenic Central Coast,
    Halfway between Los Angeles and San Francisco.

    Cayucos sits quietly between the Pacific Ocean
    And the rolling hillsides of open ranchland

    And is what some people call
    "The last of the California beach towns."

    Listen to the quiet and stillness that only
    A small town in an untouched countryside can provide.

    Cayucos is the perfect remedy
    For those who suffer from the ills and frustrations
    Of life in the fast lane in our crowded cities.

    Peaceful, underdeveloped ranchlands
    With cattle grazing on undulating, oak-crested hills
    Provide a respite for the city weary.

Childhood Home

I hadn't thought of this before,
    But as a military brat,
    Moving every year or two,
    Phil had no sense of a fixed childhood home—

    Except Cayucos.

The Best Way to Find Seaglass

Walk and talk along the beach,
   Bending over occasionally to pick up a piece,
   Whether tucked among the pebbles,
   Or even simply lying open on the sand.
   Watch for a bit of translucence or luminence,
   An unexpected shining in the water and the sun.

The Not-Best Way to Find Seaglass

Go out alone, acquisitive,
　Curious to see how bountiful the gifts from the sea may be.

　Two hours later, after forty other eager eyes searching:
　Not as bountiful as one might think.

　Or, perhaps, part of the joy was the finding
　In the midst of conversation.

A Trade

Caleb's seaglass colors were unmatched,
    Including several blues that I simply could not spot.

    Once we got home, he proposed a trade:
    One of his precious blues for one of my larger clears.

    I happily agreed, suspecting I got the better end of the bargain,
    Delighted most by the thoughtful suggestion.

Goodbye to the Sushi

I was a little surprised to find that
  Both large platters of sushi were already gone.

  Good thing we didn't hold those 144 pieces until the reception—
  They didn't store well, and were a popular item among ourselves.

Timed Excursion

Caleb and I headed out to walk the beach the other direction.

   We set the timer for 15 minutes,

   And made it back to the house at 10:15,

   Ready to get ready.

Getting Ready

Some showered.
    All changed clothes.

    Caleb's nicer flannel went missing,
    But he found it, tucked among his other clothes.

    Some wore flip-flops.
    (Phil almost did, along with a suit.)

    The cemetery was only three minutes away.
    We opted to wait as long as possible at home,

    And glimpsed the waiting crowd
    As we approached.

Funeral

After only a minute or two to greet those around us,
    Uncle Mark began.

He talked of Cheri's light,
Her smile and sweetness.

He read much of 1 Corinthians 13,
Pointing out how much this applied to Cheri.

She embodied love.
She navigated her cancer diagnosis with courage and grace.

Without amplification,
It was a bit difficult to hear every word,

But we could follow along in the programs provided.
No singing. No one else spoke.

Lucille and Douglas, Cheri's parents, already there.
Ken's ashes, too.

Now Cheri's ashes, too, put to rest.
No one stepped forward to toss on a handful of dirt.

The two employees had a system:
Bucket, bucket, bucket of dirt.

Lift headstone. Set in place.
Insert flowers into the opening.

Forty-five minutes,
Beginning to end.

Reception Set-Up

I had intended to help with the food set-up.
  But I was listening to the service intently,
  Then fell into conversation,
  So by the time we reached the church,
  All the food was out of the fridge.

  I walked into the meeting room to find
  All set up beautifully:
  The food tables, the dessert table
  (Just one cake, but a whole tray of cookies),
  All the serving utensils and drinks and napkins.

  Like a fairy godmother,
  Lisa had taken care of everything.

The Problem with Catered Food

After eating so much,
The enticement of the reception hardly appeals—
We've eaten most of it before.

But at least we held back a few surprises!

Supernaturally Preserved

No part of the food looked anything other than perfectly fresh.

(Well—one strawberry on Abraham's shortcake looked a bit frozen.)

My prayer was answered.

Not only that, but on reflection:
If we had ordered for pickup that morning,
What would I have done?

Walked away with twice what we needed?
Tried to transport this all by myself?
How long would it have taken for the staff to get me the food?

Thanks be to God for all his guidance.

Guest List

7 Lykoshes: Philip, Amy, Jadon, Isaiah, Abraham, Jonadab, Caleb.

7 Reneaus: Jennifer, Kane, Drake, Casey, his mother, his sister, his mother's friend.

2 parent Kniffens: Gail and Mark.

5 Cambria Kniffens: Steve and Lorie, Reagan, Reagan's husband, and Gehrig.

6 Reno Kniffens: Tim and Sherrill, Leah and her husband, Bethany and her husband.

2 Sacramento Kniffens: Susannah and Ruben.

5 cousin Kniffens: Jason and Justin, Kelli, and the twins.

4 distant relatives: Linda and another cousin, Arlene and Dave.

2 Placerville friends.

2 Cambria supports: Lisa and her husband.

Whole Foods Order

The Lykoshes Ate

Classic Sushi Platter with White Rice: Serves 16

Berry Chantilly Cake: Serves 20

Mediterranean Mezze Platter: Serves 16

Party Pinwheel Package: Serves 32

Cubed Meat and Cheese Platter: Serves 16

Shrimp Trio: Serves 16

Classic Deviled Eggs: Serves 16

Classic Antipasti Platter: Serves 16

The Reception Enjoyed

Strawberry Shortcake: Serves 20

Assorted Cookies: Serves 30

Mediterranean Mezze Platter: Serves 16

Party Pinwheel Package: Serves 32

Cubed Meat and Cheese Platter: Serves 16

Shrimp Trio: Serves 16

Classic Deviled Eggs: Serves 16

Wrap Platter: Serves 16

Classic Antipasti Platter: Serves 32

Fresh Fruit Platter: Serves 16

European Cheese Platter: Serves 16

Wraps

Chicken salad wraps.
    Turkey, cheese, and lettuce wraps.
    I was surprised to see, on Abraham's plate,
    A falafel wrap.

    "Wow, Abraham—did you mean to get a falafel wrap?"

    "I don't know—what is falafel?"

    A bit later, the disgruntled comment:
    "I should have known better than to get something
    With the word 'awful' in its name."

Numerous Compliments on the Food

A perfect spread.

  The right mix of foods to appeal to everyone.

  Where did you get the cake? It's so moist!

  Well done on the food!

The Best Compliment

Casey's mom's friend from Costa Rica said:
   "I have to hand it to you.
   Not only were your boys so handsome
   And well-behaved ...

   And you look like you're about eleven yourself."

One Reader Relative

Back when we were farming,

    Gramps (Philip's Grandpa Doug) would print out my blogs.

    "I know you, but you don't know me.

    I read your writing—hundreds of those pages."

Later:

"I don't know how you raised all those boys?

Were they on strict instructions to behave?"

"No—this is pretty much how they always are.

That's how I could raise them—

They are good boys."

Indeed.

Redemption

I think about how one cousin
    Was doing hardcore drugs for a season.

    Another, after his wife left him,
    Was too broken up to even see Phil
    After we got engaged.

    One clean.
    The other happily married with teens ...

    Look around to see good life change.

The Two Weeks Before the Week She Passed

I hadn't caught up with Jennifer
  Long enough to hear the story of Cheri's passing.

  Two weeks before, Gail and Mark came to visit.
  They could see that she was ailing.

  The week before, Cheri had the women from church come over.
  They gave her a prayer shawl and prayed for her.

The Week She Passed

On Monday, a friend took her to the doctor.
    She wasn't well enough for her ongoing,
    Five days in 28, into perpetuity, chemo treatment.

    She asked: "Why am I still doing chemo?"

    The doctor decided to downgrade her to chemo pills,
    Starting the following week.
    She signed (again) a Do Not Resuscitate order.

    Later in the week, she said to Jennifer: "I am ready to go.
    I'm not wanting to go, but I am ready."

The Morning She Passed

November 15, 2024, a Friday morning,
   She called Jennifer:
   "I'm having a hard time breathing."

When Jennifer arrived, she asked,
"Do you want me to call 911?"
"Yes, I think we should."

When the paramedics came,
They didn't put her on a gurney,
But took her outside in her scootabout chair.

A gentle snow had just begun to fall,
And she looked up to heaven,
A peaceful countenance.

In that moment, the Lord took her.

Of Course, Nothing Is Quite That Simple

"Did your mom have a history of seizures?"
"No!"

The paramedics started acting fast.

Jennifer said: "Stop! She has a DNR!"
And ran in to grab that paper as proof.

The paramedics took the body away.
Jennifer called Philip, in tears, traumatized.

Every death, when it comes, is a surprise.

So Much Grace

Cheri was not alone—
   She had her daughter with her.

   Jennifer was not alone—
   She had the paramedics to help.

   The paramedics had clear instructions
   On what to do, and what not to do.

   To look up at the snowflakes,
   And then behold the face of Jesus ...

   As beautiful as it could be,
   For what it was.

The Problem of Leftovers

I had an idea on what to do with
    Cubes of meat and cheese:
    Freeze overnight,
    Put in the refrigerated bag,
    Fly home.

But what about the leftover
Pinwheels and wraps and shrimp?

We sent some home with willing eaters.
The rest Steve took to his restaurant,
Convinced that his staff would eat
Anything we would send their way.

"You'd be amazed at what they eat
That is not seafood."

On the Dessert Table

Only later did I recall that
    The strawberry shortcake was meant to feed 20,
    Not 45.
    Ah, well.

    One piece remained.

    Who am I going to call?

    Jadon!

Early Release

I had expected the reception to run until 3pm,
    With a vague conception about cleaning up afterwards.

    Nope! We were fully done by 2:15
    Building clean and emptied.

    All of my boys had made their way home already,
    But I drove back, full of thanksgiving.

    A really lovely reception,
    And now time to be free.

The Afternoon

Phil took a nap.
  Maybe a few others did, too.

  I worked on the puzzle,
  Wanting to verify that all the pieces were going to make it home

  (Some had gotten stuck on the tablecloth—
  Which probably wouldn't be a big deal, but it's good to check).

  A peaceful few hours until Jadon said,
  "I'm hungry."

Desired Birthday Dinner

Phil wanted fish and chips for his birthday dinner.
    We headed to Morro Bay,
    To Dutchman's Seafood House.

    Five of us had fish and chips
    Including me—first time since, I think, spring of 2020.
    Abraham and Caleb had burgers and fries.

    We mentioned our family preference for condiments,
    And received four extra containers of tartar sauce.
    I gave a third of the fish to Jadon.

The Bonus Second

Unaccountably, Phil ordered
    The Pepsi version of Sprite, Starry.

"Really?" I said in surprise.
"I've never seen you drink that!"

With his first swallow, he made a face:
"Sweet."

He couldn't finish it, so he passed it to Isaiah,
The only one with a desire to try it.

Then he went to the bathroom.
I had been keeping an eye on the various wait staff.

One near the door had looked to be working hard,
And when our eyes met, I smiled. Always good to work hard.

He came over, asked Isaiah what he was drinking,
And brought him another.

It was so sudden and unexpected,
I didn't utter a word of protest.

But Phil teased me when I came back—
Smiling at other men, on his birthday, while he stepped out.

How to Eat Fish and Chips

You can just eat a bite.

    Or eat it with tartar sauce.

    Or pour malt vinegar on (for a bit of flavor).

    Or squeeze lemon juice.

    Or any mix of the above.

    French fries, too, can be thus treated.

Heading Back

We hurried home.
   I pulled out the cheesecake,
   Pulled out the candles 5-2,
   Decided against lighting them,
   Set the cake on the front corner of the table ...
   Only to wait and wait.

   Jadon checked Find My Friends.
   Phil, with Isaiah and Joe,
   Had stopped at Uncle Mark and Aunt Gail's.

The Birthday Song

No candles to blow out,
   The song sung at different tempos ...
   It was not the cleanest performance,
   But at least we got it done.

   Phil missed the five minute rehearsal,
   As Abraham and Jadon practiced
   How slowly they could sing it,
   Creatively incorporating multiple verses of,
   "And many more"—

So slowly that those four syllables
Became more like forty.

I took one for the team,
Listening to that rehearsal.

Storebought Cheesecake

Even though the cake looked beautiful,
  The bits I tried didn't compare to my own,
  So I skipped a slice.
  Caleb, still full from dinner, skipped too.

Second Time Through

Golden hour triumph.
 Gorgeous glow of the puzzle.
 No pieces missing.

Sitting in an Adirondack Chair

One side of the house's wraparound porch
    Had Adirondack chairs—the side away from the wind.
    I determined to enjoy this gift, too,
    Even briefly.

    The quiet, wind-free indoors proved
    An easier environment to read.

Just not quite as unique.

Last Sunset in the House

All of us awake,
    Watching again as the sun sank low,
    This time obscured by clouds far above the horizon,
    So there was no real sense of sunset,
    Other than a fading of the intensity of the glow—
    But how long since we saw the outline of the sun?

Impossible to say.

Clouds make clear things hazy.

Heading to Bed

At 8pm, I went to bed,
    Surprised to find the moon
    Perfectly framed in
    The skylight above me.

Saturday, April 5, 2025

Not Feeling Well

I woke with a screaming sore throat and stuffy nose.
  I took remedies and tried again to sleep.

I rested in bed until 5:15am,
When Bob sent the signal for prayer.

I was so out of it, I walked into the door to the garage—
I hadn't thought to turn the flashlight on in time.

I managed the full hour,
Then abruptly got off.

If I had to estimate my vitality:
Twenty percent.

Change of Plans

I had ordered Hearst Castle tickets for 11am,

    Thinking: this is like 2pm in Virginia.

    Of course we'll be ready to go!

    But why leave our marvelous house a minute sooner than necessary?

    Gorgeous view, plenty of bathrooms,

    Boys happy to play games, space to lie down.

    The website wasn't cooperative to easily swap tickets,

    So I set my phone alarm for 8am,

    And called as soon as they opened.

    After waiting on hold for five minutes that felt like an hour,

    I managed to change our Designing the Dream tour time to 1pm,

    The only other time with seven spots available that day.

The Trio, Second Day

Caleb and I, better equipped to know what to look for,
    Set out on a mission.
    The tide was still high when we set out,
    So we were the first on the beach.
    He found something like four blue pieces in a row.

    I eventually found a single blue bit, the size of a tiny bead.

The Trio, Second Day

I ordered
    Three croissants,
    One almond croissant,
    Three blueberry muffins,
    One strawberry scone, and
    One gluten-free lemon scone.

    Lisa had recommended this shop,
    So we would try it out.

Same Order at the Coffee Shop

Though I was not feeling awesome,
  The idea of a chai sounded good.

  But I hadn't considered the challenge
  Of holding cup and pastry box,

  Then trying to pick up seaglass and
  Put in the proper pocket.

  Phil carried the box,
  As we slowly strolled down the beach.

  Eventually Phil left us behind,
  Carrying the hoard alone.

Caleb Went to His Happy Place

Caleb found a part of the beach that was exceptionally promising.

    With our house in view in the distance,

    He found three pieces in about five seconds,

    Then scoured more carefully.

    Eventually I had to leave him behind.

    I wanted to take photos of details,

    And needed to clean out the kitchen,

    Ensure we had packed all we needed to pack.

    I left the keen-eyed treasure hunter with regrets.

Old Mother Hubbard Redux

I went to get some pinwheels for breakfast,
    And was stunned to find all gone but about 24 vegetable ones.
    Although I initially put them in bags, I soon tossed them.

    A few shrimp remained, no longer smelling the freshest,
    So I threw away perhaps twenty.

    The half tubs of hummus met a similar demise.

    We ate six of the twelve remaining deviled eggs,
    But they were slimy in feel and not flavorful, so I threw them away,
too.

    The rest of the cheesecake happily went.
    The ice cream was already gone.

    I would never have guessed that my family could eat through
    A full $850 in catered food in little more than 48 hours.

    With an empty cupboard, we would soon need food.

One Last Beach Treasure Hunt

Once most of the last-minute chores were done,
    I headed to the beach once more to look for seaglass.

    I had some modest success.
    A man who looked like Paul Perez (from Guam or Hawaii)

    Handed me a clear piece.
    I had made no eye contact, nor noticed him.

    Perhaps he was an angel.
    He asked what color I was looking for.

    "Blue."
    "Oh. Yes. That's one of the hardest to come by."

    He walked away, then said,
    "Ma'am? Here's a green piece for you."

It's Always More Than You Think

I was back to the house with twenty minutes before departure.

We used every one of those minutes.

Lunch

Fairy godmother Lisa had recommended
    A few restaurants in town,
    And he had been working our way through.

    Hidden Kitchen was our destination,
    But when we drove past,
    An actual crowd of people was out front.

    We parked and went instead into
    The dive Mexican restaurant behind the gas station.

    It was over $100 for the seven of us,
    But the burritos, when they came, were so massive
    They covered lunch and late lunch.

    My Cayucos Burrito include French fries,
    And it tasted great, but in the future I would consider
    Phil's breakfast burrito with steak,
    Or Jadon's loaded fries.

Location, Location, Location

We drank our Jalliscos and ate
    Under the statue "The Great Communicators,"
    Of two dolphins cavorting.

    Then we walked the pier,
    As I carried a heavy bag ... all the lunch leftovers.

On the Road Up to San Simeon

On California 1:

Beautiful blue water,

A few parking sites with small trails,

Rolling cattle lands with a few black cows,

Harmony: Population 18,

A surprisingly vigorous protest in tiny Cambria (later I realized: part of the Hands Off! national protest, which explains the angry vehemence),

A few palm trees,

One red Spanish colonial, with red tile roof,

One RV heading south (which reminded me of all the pent-up frustration of driving to a national park in a car, behind an RV).

The Visitor Center

The indoor toilets were out of order,
   So we made use of port-a-potties.
   When we signed in, we were told we had a
   Twenty-five minute wait to catch our bus.

   So I read display signs, and watched the time.

On the Bus

We expected the bus to be full,
   So headed to the back.
   The boys sat in all five seats.

   But the bus was far from full,
   So we spread out.

Not My Favorite

Hearst Castle: one of thirteen estates
    Of one of the world's wealthiest men,
    A ridiculous assemblage of tacky art
    And cobbled together styles,
    Designed to impress.

    He would violate the Jewish ethical code,
    By having workmen tear out something
    They had just finished.

    His two year little project
    Turned into a 28-year monstrosity,
    Unfinished at the time of his death.

    The whole place reeks of unhappiness and sin.
    Nothing to be envious of.

One Tour Was Enough

What a blessing to have signed up for only one small tour.
  Back down the mountain,
  The views were magnificent,
  But we were done.

  We ate our leftover lunch
  And shared pastries in the parking lot.

A Quick Stop in San Simeon

Jennifer wanted photos of the cousins,
  So we stopped by to take a few.
  Casey didn't look up when we entered,
  An indicator of how out of it he is.

  We went down to the ocean briefly:
  No seaglass, and soft, pebbly sand.

  We headed out soon.

A Quick Stop in Cayucos

Phil and Joe said goodbye,
    And headed south to Lake Arrowhead.

    I had been feeling sick to my stomach—
    Too much nastiness with Hearst, perhaps—
    So we walked the beach for a bit,
    Then headed to the airport.

Goodbye for Now

Our plane took off around 7:15pm.
    From my seat, I could see the unvisited coast to the south.
    Then the plane turned, and I could see Morro Rock,
    And the more familiar bay.

    Though I couldn't see the sun itself,
    It tickled me that I was getting the airborne glimpse
    Of one last orange California sunset ...
    An unanticipated final gift.

I Think Cheri Would Have Loved It

Happy family,

    Beautiful location,

    Lots of good food,

    Low-key responsibilities,

    Joy and laughter,

    Even (a bit, at times) a vacation feel.

Made in the USA
Columbia, SC
10 April 2025

56431586R00093